Ambush

Silvia Curbelo

MAIN STREET RAG PUBLISHING COMPANY
CHARLOTTE, NC

ISBN: 1-930907-62-1

Main Street Rag
4416 Shea Lane
Charlotte, NC 28227
www.MainStreetRag.com

Acknowledgements:

American Poetry Review: "Before the Long Silence," "Garden Party," "Hearing the News," "Birthday Song," "Learning to Play Coltrane," "Not This," "Jessica Gone," "Shine," "Headache," "The Law of Supply and Demand."
Bloomsbury Review: "This Poem is Missing."
Crab Orchard Review: "The Visitors."
Gettysburg Review: "In the Land of Missed Chances," "Ambush."
Notre Dame Review: "Fifteen," "Barcarole."
Tiferet: "Faith."

Some of the poems in this collection also appear in the following anthologies:

Birthday Poems: A Celebration (Thunder's Mouth Press, 2002).
Snakebird: Thirty Years of Anhinga Poets (Anhinga Press, 2004).
You Drive Me Crazy: Love Poems for Real Life (Warner Books, 2004).
Never Before (Four Way Books, 2005).

I'm grateful to The Florida Division of Cultural Affairs, the Cintas Foundation, the Tampa/Hillsborough County Arts Council and the Writer's Voice for generous fellowships, to the Seaside Institute's "Escape to Create" program for valuable time to write, and especially to Scott Douglass and his hard-working Main Street Rag. Heartfelt thanks also to Aubrey Hampton, Susan Hussey, Sharry Smith and Pam Rubenstein for endless support, to Anna Tomczak for constant inspiration, and to Melissa Fair and Rhonda J. Nelson for their great critical eye. And most of all, to Tom and to Adrian for making things right.

Contents

Before the Long Silence

Some words open dark wings
inside us. They carry us off
in the telling, the air going on
beyond language, beyond breath.

It's the small moments
that change everything.
On the last night my father
woke from a long, restless sleep
and pointed to a corner
of the room. *A bird,* he said.

You'd think it would be easy, living.
All you need is a fistful of earth, a boat, a nest, a jail,
a little breath, some drops of blood, and longing.
— Adam Zagajewski

The Visitors

They stand without pity or shame
like tourists on the bridge to your next
great sadness. They have been walking
in bad shoes. They want a cold beer.

They've come with their one small
suitcase, and night's implausible
laundry list. It's late.
They're tired of being poor.

All day the wind fails them, so does
the sky unloosening its sullen
Esperanto. They know the hard
currency of coffee and cheap cigarettes,

the accidental prayer of rain
on a car roof. Priests of indecision
and poor judgment, they reach into
the ancient dark to pull a coin out of thin air.

Call it a gift, a simple benediction,
as they move tenderly through the door
of your best life, whispering
Take it, it's yours. Write this down.

—*for Ann*

In the Land of Missed Chances

There was no news
in God's country. The sun
sank without warning.
Every ship sailed away.

No one sang for her supper
or looked for answers in the stars
or prayed for rain.
No one poured the last wine.
The dispossessed left nothing
in their wake.

There were no telephones
ringing, no music playing.
Nothing bloomed in the yard.
No one was lost or blamed
or left for dead.

There were no crimes to speak of.
The cops found no fresh signs
of struggle, no blood on
the sheets, no lipstick-smeared
cigarettes still smoldering in
ashtrays. No one gave up
the ghost or fell from grace.

Nobody rolled the dice
or held the winning card.
The last of our luck ran out,
swallowed the key
and closed the book.
We didn't have a prayer.

Hearing the News

It is like fire.
It is a kind of burning.
Silence moves through it
like breath. It goes nowhere.
Where it begins it
ends, a notion surrounding
itself like a ring of flame.
It is nothing you have not heard before.
It is the essence of sound.
Imagine yourself there, not
there. It is the light falling
without you through trees
whose voicelessness
embodies the idea of you,
a burning thing among trees.
The way without you nothing
speaks and nothing
answers. Someone who is not
named, who is not there. Or
something that falls and is
not heard for many years,
but whose name is a constant,
a whisper of itself
among trees. The way
a child might imagine his own
death, distant and luminous
as a star. And burning.

This Poem is Missing

The difference between a mountain
and an abyss is a question of perspective.

Every mirror is an island
we're rowing toward.

Look how this moment disappears behind a cloud.
I never said the world was substantial.

Even as it conceals it,
the glove imitates the hand.

The air around a flower
is also the flower.

A basket of roses speaks for itself.
Silence is another thing altogether.

If nothing falls in the forest
does it matter who isn't there to listen?

Sorrows outnumber trees.
A man drinks to his orphaned heart

and swallows the voice
of what is missing.

The poem inside the mirror is
no dream, but tell me,

who will console the dreamer?

Fall

It was a wing, it was a kiss,
soft as a word, or as breath
in the middle of a word, it moved
through the air like smoke then fell
as quietly and deliberately
as any falling thing, a word,
a wing, a leaf, or sunlight
falling through leaves, heavier
than air, the way music
falls sometimes, or wind
after a storm has cleared
But it was softer than that,
like new snow falling
on the still-green grass by the side
of the road, or a certain kind of silence
I thought I saw clouds in the distance,
I thought I saw an olive tree,
or a birch, maybe
I thought there was wind
and branches moving overhead
and the birds knew me
It was a wing, a word, a blade, a kiss
It was a song, it was a kind of singing
as if somewhere someone was singing
and I could hear the air moving
through it, that perfect rushing sound
like blood rushing over bone
But it was more than breath, more than
music really, the vestige of some
elemental language suspended

in space, then falling the way a leaf
falls, or a voice, any voice
I thought it called out to me
I thought it said my name
in the pure reverence of light
and air, right where I stood,
the rain sinking its small
bright teeth into the earth
But it wasn't rain, it was not
that kind of falling, not
rain, not a stone, never a stone
though I could feel the weight of it
the way a stone has weight
and texture, and language, and a voice
And if I leaned my ear against
the trembling mouth of it
I could hear my own name softly
falling, a shining, falling thing
like a coin or a wish, it was
that real, it was in the air,
still falling

Garden Party

The day makes its final appearance,
the sky rubbed out in places
with a blue so understated it's nearly
a memory of blue. Forget the vase
arranged on the table, the tulips
are too vague. Even the white
tablecloth is an erasure.
Imagine the pale drone
of dinner conversation,
the politics of brie, cold soup.
The good china infects everything.
Even now the knife falters,
the wine glass can't be saved.
Think of the blank mirrors
of spoons, the fish
whose whiteness is a given.
Consider the ravenous napkin.

Ambush

The room. The white piano.
The stars gone slack.
The unmistakable rising up
to meet her. In heels and
a dark suit. A green light. A wing.
An accomplice. Silence and
more. Not silence. The mandolin still
trembling, still holding its moan.
Scar of light on the page. The blade
of an old story. The hand, the voice,
the deep pocket. Whatever stars are left.
The map, the spit and polish.
The sky like a great pond.
The drift. The notion.
The wine with its warm hide.
The lavish hand grenade. The stars and more.
The cloud, its soft harness.
The well. The wound. The warning.

Birthday Song

The day I was born I was
born screaming, weren't we all,
and who's to say there was no reason
to crawl headfirst into that vastness,
the great cathedral of what if.
I was alone and wanting and pissed off.
I felt the wind moving through it,
the sheer fact of desire entering
me like a long breath, obvious
as candlelight and cheap wine,
while happiness insinuated itself,
little flaws in the flesh.
Then one day it's ten minutes past the time
anything matters, and someone
is stepping closer through
the music, cutting slow circles
across the bright prairie
of dancing, moving among the loud
shirts and soft eyes of the newly lost.
And I can feel myself falling
like hard luck, like some poor excuse
for rain, or every notion that takes me
unawares, miles from everything,
knowing full well whatever fate
befalls me, gravity takes me
by the heart and sleeve.
Imagine a bed made for such
forced landings, the slow tumble
out of our own survival instincts, feathers
and grief, night falling where it will,

going down like barometric pressure,
while life plays like a blue movie
on somebody's dirty little bedroom wall.
And love still shines like the hall light
across those perfect ruins, a train
wreck of misspent youth and joy,
and doing it all over, with anyone,
while spread eagle loneliness
rubs its sore ankles on God's
infernal kitchen floor, black
square, white
square, the music careening over
everything broken, and rising,
and newly born.
Imagine someone moving closer
through that music, shrugging off
the wings, unbuttoning
the losses, then bending to touch
the tender corners of the cloth,
thinking how easily
we could erase the years
gleaming on the table
with one eternal breath of praise
that puts out each small fire
as if it were a wish
and we were singing.

Fifteen

Soot in the eye of the beholder.
In the branches of sleep,

in the room's perfect hive,
incomprehension catches fire.

His youth like a strange song
deep in his throat.

From her mother's abandoned
picture books

gardenias hum, their pale
green scent empty as a door.

Knowing is not responsibility.
A feeling not unlike ash beneath her tongue.

Through a forest of wings
the television answers.

Everywhere the trees burn.
Who can understand such longing?

Rubble of words and leaves.
A boy fumbles through dark pockets.

A girl lights a cigarette.
And the match blows.

Learning to Play Coltrane

She thought it was green, not
the emerald green of Indian summer
but a green like a darkening plain,
or the shadow rivers cast.
She thought it was light, a glint
or a warning, the shine
at the papery edge
of storm clouds. The way
a voice rising and falling becomes
a premonition, a dampness
at the back of her neck. Or maybe
it was more of an imprint,
a memory of sound, some afternoon
after the circus has left town
and all that remains is a field
strewn with garbage, a music
of pasted stars and ruin.
And she thought of a color
like that, mud-green, the green
of a small sadness, shapeless
as the wind itself. And for a moment
she owned everything inside it,
the light, the field, the wind.

—for Adrian

Not This

It's not the way the light haunts
that particular landscape, or how clouds

in the distance imitate the world at rest.
The way the curtains hold the late

afternoon is not an issue. It's not
the lilies abandoned on the table,

or the dog lying beside her, or the wine.
It's not the weight of memory

on his eyelids. It's not the empty cup
he carries walking home in the dark

through fields brimming with sleep,
or the precarious raft of her

mouth on his, or her hands
in the evenings

putting cold cream
where her youth had been.

Jessica Gone

Silence lifting the latch,
unbuttoning the dress, fingering
scarves that wind as
the road winds.
The cut roses understand
there's safety in numbers.
Someone ladles soup
into a bowl. Someone
touches the black hair,
the single gardenia
helpless as a love letter,
prayer, snow on the ground.

— for Jane

Faith

Sunday morning empty
as two stones, tethered
to nothing
Empty as a room
or a face undone
by memory
like a song the wind
carries
then lets go
Empty as letting go

Emptiness of wind
across the valley
and the rain that falls without
astonishment
on the bare grass
Emptiness of grass, then
and of roads going back
to the start
A map, a bridge, a canvas, a shore

or waves released
against that shore
Or a landscape touched
by nothing
anchored to nothing
Not a harbor
but a story, a bandage, a voice

Shine

The day seemed strangely
out of context, black and white
as our hearts. We hated the smell
of sunlight in the alleys, the ruined
voices on TV. We couldn't read
between the lines. We craved
meaning and sleep, a hole
swallowing a hole.
Elsewhere there were trees,
there were sidewalks
and food. We had music and
cigarettes and cars, the ownership
of light and noise, loneliness, air.
As if a boy had smashed open
all the windows. As if
the ashen sky meant rain
and nothing more. At night
we saw dogs rooting in the shadows,
and men walking in the cold,
their hands drifting out of warm
pockets reaching for what? Solace?
A match? Imagine something
shines in the dark and something
moves towards that small
brightness. Haven't you
ever touched someone
in just that way?

A Short History of Silence

The grass tells nothing.
The sky sits in its simple
cage of days. No sound
like the past blowing through.

Only the wind knows what's
at stake here, moving into
the scenery, running at the mouth.
Hush, say the daylilies

shaking their heads a bit.
Silence is its own music,
soft as dirt. No one notices
the orphan drift of clouds,

the wingtip scar of the horizon
balanced between nowhere
and this. *Hush*,
whisper the azaleas.

But nothing's as wordless
as a young girl standing on the lawn
waving her handkerchief, wind
unraveling her damp hair.

Headache

I woke up in a strange place,
in a dream, in a nest of fireflies.
When I opened my eyes I was
in a garden splintered by sunlight,
red roses seeped through the pale
leaves and the grass hummed.
The tepid air filled my lungs
like music, something French
and sentimental. I wanted
to sing, and why not?
I thought I was still dreaming.
I wanted a cigarette, a bath,
a glass of milk.
There was a small city behind my eyes
with roads and trees and newspapers.
I could feel it clanking to life,
its dogs and cars and crusty loaves
of bread, its bicycles and
postage stamps, its hundred
excuses for living, black coffee, rain.
It was a Monday or a Thursday,
I'm sure of it, and daylight
lay across my eyes like a net
of blunt knives. I wanted to wash
the bright taste of sunlight
from my tongue, I wanted sleep,
I wanted an answer.
My life was a dull museum,
a magazine, an accident
of fashion, rakish and foolish

as a white silk scarf. I was in a garden,
I could hear bells tolling across
fields, across churchyards and
parking lots. I could hear couples
breathing in their cars, old men
in park benches, I could hear lilacs
blooming, radios, bees.
I wanted to bask in the harsh light
of possibility. I wanted to lie on a red velvet
couch under a skylight, to lose all sense
of proportion and live without pity or
blame, without a trace of irony.
I wanted wind and all its
consequences, leaves
in my hair, and honey, not sugar,
for my tea. I wanted absolution,
I wanted an aspirin.
I wanted to nail all the windows open,
to memorize each searing blade
of light, each speeding train
between the eyes, each brooding
way the body answers, the soft and
crooked places where the bones meet and sing.

Barcarole

In dreams the music never
fails us. It spins and swirls,

a woman's glittery skirt,
and our unhappy childhoods

rise into sudden air
like so many small birds.

Beneath the drift and pull of memory
a boy climbs a tree.

Hand over fist, the truth follows.
Something rattles the shadows.

A ripple, a small breeze
lifting the palest hair.

The way a stranger might touch
a careful finger to his lips

just as the boy lets go of the branch.

The Law of Supply and Demand

The pawn shops of the world are offering
their wares. Sunlight pours in

through the single window and it's
enough to know the sky goes on.

The street is ancient, it fends for itself.
Some are turned away hungry.

In a world of closed doors
something is unlatched and left

for broken. Whatever it takes,
there's a need and a cost.

The sky with its hundred false starts
where the nearly possible meets

the hopelessly undone,
the one promise it keeps.

Someone holds out the future
in his hands like a piece of bread.

Open this, he says.

Notes

"Not This," "Barcarole" and "The Law of Supply and Demand" are based on large format Polaroid transfers by artist Anna Tomczak.

"Learning to Play Coltrane" is for Adrian Errico.

"The Visitors" and "Faith" are loosely based on a series of email conversations with novelist Ann Darby about the writing process.

"Jessica Gone" is dedicated to Jane Nobel Maxwell.